READ

BETWEEN

the LINES

Read Between the Lines

Windows of Recourse: Provocative Essays for Saving Our Children

by Dr. Charles L. Singleton

Edited by Janet A. Cook and Lauren J. Emerson

Designed by Elaine Streithof

First Edition 1997.

Published by The Singleton Press.

Printed in the United States of America.

Second Edition 2019.

Literary Technical Consultants: Tahesha Brown and Lavata Pollard

Published by Allenco Publishing Inc., Atlanta, GA.

Printed in the United States of America.

Read Between the Lines

Windows of Recourse: Provocative Essays for Saving Our Children

by Dr. Charles L. Singleton

In the words of the estimable clinical and educational consultant and journalist, Dr. Charles L. Singleton, "Children are gifts to the world and our greatest resource for replicating man's existence and improving his future." And, as *Read Between the Lines* reveals, many educators and parents have seemingly forgotten just how precious children are. Today, the needs of young people are too often overlooked, and we tend to frequently forget how susceptible and vulnerable they are to the crippling effects of violence, suicide, drugs, broken families, gangs, peer pressure, and the ever-increasing perils of social media.

Parents and educators have an inherent and genuine responsibility to provide today's young people with steadfast opportunities, safe and nurturing environments, and a strong sense of self so that our children may succeed in both their personal and professional lives. Absolutely, there are no easy answers to the plethora of problems, Dr. Singleton illuminates; nevertheless, the essays in *Read Between the Lines* get us started on the right path.

For over 50 years, Dr. Singleton's informative essays have appeared in numerous publications, including the *Atlanta Journal-Constitution* (AJC), *USA Today*, *CoolKids Magazine*, the *Champion* newspaper, *CrossRoadNews*, *Applied Scholastics*, *Georgia Association of Health, Physical Education, Recreation, and Dance (GAHPERD) Journal*, and the *Family Journal, USA & Overseas*. His articles and writings over the years have been published both locally and nationally; occasionally overseas, and frequently shared with 650,000+ Facebook fans, Twitter followers, news blogs, and various other social media, such as Instagram,

LinkedIn, Google+, Pinterest, Next Door, Legacy.com, and 1.3 million-plus viewers of Southeast Queens Scoop Blog-Streetwise Digital News (SQSBSDN), and various businesses and affiliates. One such article and fitness manual, at the Atlanta VA Center for Visual & Neurocognitive Rehabilitation (CVNR) Aging and Motor Decline study 2015, is still trending.

Educational

Paperback

101 pages

$19.95

Order your copy of *Read Between the Lines* at Allenco Publishing Inc., Atlanta, GA. It is also available globally, including at Barnes & Noble and on Amazon.

DEDICATION

These compositions are dedicated to my loving parents, Mr. Clement Addison Singleton Sr. and the late Mrs. Catherine Flood-Singleton of Summerville, South Carolina, and to my son, Chase, whose strength and courage inspired me to complete this book.

My special thanks to you, the reader.

READ

WINDOWS OF RECOURSE

BETWEEN

Provocative Essays for

the LINES

Saving Our Children

by

CHARLES L. SINGLETON, EdD

ABOUT THE AUTHOR

D r. Charles Louis Singleton was born and raised in Summerville, South Carolina. He earned his Bachelor of Science degree from Elizabeth City State University in North Carolina in 1968, a master of arts degree from Atlanta University in Atlanta, Georgia, in 1972, and a doctor of education degree from Nova Southeastern University in Fort Lauderdale, Florida, in 1993. He also completed several courses relating to his profession, earning certificates and recognition for his efforts. He has been an education consultant since January 1981.

Dr. Singleton has received numerous awards, honors, and certificates of distinction, including Teacher of the Year (three times); YWCA Certificate of Appreciation for service; Honorary Life Membership—Georgia PTA; and Outstanding Volunteer Leadership Award—YWCA; to name a few.

He also served his country in the Vietnam War and was honorably discharged in 1971.

Dr. Singleton has been published in numerous communicational media. He is clearly recognized as a leader in his field. Historically, the Atherton Elementary Physical Education Program (Decatur, Georgia), directed by Dr. Charles L. Singleton, was recognized by both the Atlanta Paralympic Organizing Committee and the Youth and Education Program of the Atlanta Committee for the Olympic Games for its outstanding Olympic-related learning experiences (1994–1996). Dr. Singleton developed educational strategies for incorporating the goals of the Olympic movement into the classroom while matriculating at NOVA Southeastern University.

TABLE OF CONTENTS

In my opinion,

WE MUST EDUCATE

THE *total* CHILD.

INTRODUCTION

How today's society affects the education of America's young people will determine the course of human history for generations to come.

One of the most important goals of education is to instruct and to educate young people in becoming responsible citizens. Education is an invaluable resource because its tenets enable people to develop cognitively, physically, socially, and emotionally on an individual basis. In addition, an effective educational curriculum promotes individual growth and development by providing students with the opportunities to acquire moral values, social skills, and health-related fitness.

The maturation process of young people is developmental in nature. The process covers a period of growth from birth through early adulthood (0–21). However, each person's developmental timetable is unique and completely different. Through the influence of genetics, parenting, socialization, gender, and environment, one individual may evolve with adequate life skills necessary for successful integration into society. In contrast, however, another person of the very same age can develop such unacceptable behavioral traits as insolence, defiance, violence, disruption, disrespectfulness, and indolence. These inappropriate behavioral mechanisms frequently leave the person poorly prepared for a productive life. It is the author's intent that the provocative essays that follow will help to inform and educate readers about the pressing need to save our children.

1

READ

WINDOWS *of*

RECOURSE

The Atrocious Language of Youth:
VULGARISM

Many young people in our technological society are speaking nonstandard English by showing an extreme disregard for the basic rules of grammar. Simply stated, the verbal communication among some of America's youth is an atrocity.

It is a commonplace and everyday occurrence to hear children use double negatives and unacceptable sentence structures: "can't never," "don't have no," "I didn't do nothing," "you is going," "I seen her/him yesterday," "you was," "nohow am I going to help you." Moreover, the colloquial and nonstandard language of youngsters today is inundated with distasteful boos and hisses, unpleasant expletives, and profanity.

It is annoying, disdainful, and appalling to listen to young people talk when they use vulgar slang, abusive acronyms, and despicable abbreviations (e.g., MF, GD, SOB, N-word). Generally speaking, the language of an unspecified number of youths in this age of global communication is harsh, loud, and offensive. Such rhetoric goes beyond colloquialism. Seemingly, the familiar conversations of this parade of young individuals may represent the scurrilous language and thoughts of future adult generations. Such nonconforming linguists could also face insurmountable difficulties when they apply for jobs.

Like it or not, the use of appropriate English is essential for all American citizens to function successfully in today's expanding multicultural world. Worldwide, a majority of people are moving toward mastering the intricacies of speaking the English language correctly. Therefore, America's young people must seek to improve their verbal and writing skills. Entrance to future job markets will require a blending of knowledgeable skills and communication abilities. Yes, young people, your jobs and careers will continue to go to foreigners if you do not learn and apply standard English to everything you say and do.

In order to develop a person's ability to learn standard English, I strongly suggest that parents, educators, and academicians encourage young people to bowdlerize or eliminate objectionable words and phrases when speaking. Even Thomas Bowdler, the English editor, had to edit William Shakespeare's plays.

Likewise, today, the producers of rap and hip-hop music must do more thorough editing of their lyrics and musical compositions. The esoteric messages of these vocal expressions are frequently infused with the usage of improper grammar and the ongoing utterances of obnoxiousness.

Finally, etymologists, soothsayers, and the citizenry of America would probably agree that all of us, linguistically, could do a great deal to make modern English more user-friendly by expurgating obscene words and phrases from our own conversations. We must save our children's educational careers and futures by teaching them that vulgarity is crude language and needs to be removed from everyday usage. Emphatically to this point, the anomaly related to vulgarism or tothe common vernacular has to be corrected in young voices during this topsy-turvy time in human history. Now, "What language are your children learning and speaking?"

Excellence in Education:
A RATIONALE FOR THE ENHANCEMENT OF ELEMENTARY PHYSICAL EDUCATION

Excellence in education may be defined as the mastery of available knowledge through various academic performances or displays. Without doubt or uncertainty, today's students should be able to:

Speak properly; write legibly; read for understanding; complete basic mathematical problems; comprehend economics; manage money; appreciate different types of music; show abilities to recreate, socialize, interpret history, learn science; use computers; and maintain an acceptable level of physical fitness.

However, boasting and bragging about "the best schools" becomes trivial when compared to the true potential of each child. It is a shame in this period of human history that some educators, parents, and citizens measure the value of education by one standard—intellectual achievement. Those supporters who continue to use this value for determining a well-rounded child are promoting a myth.

Excellence in education must stress the true importance and worth of the total child. John Locke, the English philosopher, maintained that a newborn infant (neonate) comes into the world with a "tabula rasa" or blank mind. According to Locke, when children are environmentally stimulated through their five senses, they learn the properties of life through intellectual, physical, social, and emotional development. Therefore, elementary school curriculums must include a variety of physical activities for children.

Elementary physical education represents an essential part of general education by teaching the basic skills of proper body movement, health-related fitness, and personal safety. An appropriately designed physical education program for school-age pupils (early childhood, middle childhood, and early adolescence) can significantly enhance levels of individual fitness while increasing students' opportunities for maturational success. An effective elementary physical education program educates the entire child by promoting cultural aspects of sports, positive physical development, emotional maturity, and psychosocial needs. In conjunction with satisfying human growth and developmental requirements, a well-defined and structured physical education program will contribute to educating the total individual by influencing the process of whole learning. As a result, a positive person is created and a productive lifestyle emerges to benefit mankind.

Unfortunately, some school systems will try to resolve their funding predicaments by eliminating physical education programs and related curriculums. In my work as an education consultant/journalist, I strongly urge parents and advocates who are genuinely concerned about improving the learning environment of children to attend public hearings regarding school budget issues.

Pen-Pencil-Paper Technology:
STILL AN EDUCATIONAL CHALLENGE

Every ten seconds of the school day a student drops out of school.
— Children's Defense Fund: Moments in America

T oday in our fast-paced, technological culture, it is common to see and read about the so-called information age; an age in which we find many school districts across the United States attempting to change their curriculums by teaching and by using state-of-the-art computer technology (including computer-aided instruction, Internet systems, and electronics). Unfortunately for a number of school-age children, the mastery in developing good writing skills still remains a very difficult challenge. Granted, anyone who learns on a computer has already attained a marvelous accomplishment. Having the capability to process and access timely information contributes significantly to his or her power to learn. However, too many of our school-age youngsters today have a pressing need to continually practice the art of fundamental writing and expression (pen-pencil-paper technology).

Historically speaking, writing is a man-made technology (a form of language) that was invented approximately 8,000 years ago. Writing allows people to record language and process bits of information for human application. Furthermore, written works by various authors over the centuries have helped preserve some of mankind's most prolific achievements and enhanced civilizations on Earth. What is my point?

As an educator, I am suggesting that today's learners must turn aggressively toward developing their writing skills in order to better use modern technologies. Without a doubt, pupils with good penmanship will greatly increase their knowledge about technologies by becoming legible writers. Pityingly, some young people in our society today, regardless of having attended public schools for twelve years, simply cannot write legibly. This lack of writing skills among youth is an absolute tragedy! How can we expect these up-and-coming adults to become computer-literate when they do not know the basic principles of writing and grammar? Believe it or not, some high school seniors—following their commencement—could very well face the sequent scenario: a highly complex computerized reality for which they lack sufficient writing skills.

One solution to the dilemma, or thought-provoking supposition being perceived, is an increased emphasis on students (K–12) having more practice with pen-pencil-paper technology. I strongly believe that writing is an effective pathway to improving a learner's aptitude for using acceptable language and information. According to author Thomas Armstrong in *Seven Kinds of Smart* (1993), every human being has a "writer's voice" or "inner speech" which provides a quantum amount of thoughts for the purpose of generating human expression. Moreover, Russian psychologist Lev Semenovich Vygotsky (1896–1934) suggested that thoughts, words, and language are interdependent components of one's ability to learn and to think. Therefore, we must teach our children how to sketch out their visions and write about these mental images on paper.

And who knows; a young writer just might compose a manuscript worthy of worldly acclaim. As points of reference, history reminds us that poetess Phillis Wheatley (1753–1784), an American prodigy at age fourteen, impressively caught the attention of the citizenry of the United States with her articles and poem "To His Excellency, General Washington." Whereas Thomas Edison (1847–1931), an American inventor with only three months of formal education, successfully managed his deafness and produced for the world more than 1,300 patents, and also gave mankind electronics and light in special ways.

The juxtaposition of Phillis Wheatley and Thomas Edison, along with my personal experience of observing how children learn, motivates me to believe that "the pen is mightier than the sword" (Edward Bulwer-Lytton); and possibly the computer. Now please try to understand me. The computer is an excellent supplemental invention, and it will be with us for the millennial years to come. However, we must not totally depend on the computer, due to its susceptibility to drawbacks—electrical problems, affordability limitations, the dubious authenticity of documents, the availability of reliable data, breaches of confidentiality, opportunities for criminal activity, etc. These and other unavoidable circumstances are influences to consider.

Emphatically speaking, the present era has been called an age of science, technology, and information. It is certainly all of these descriptive landscapes and more. This moment in human existence is indeed an age for writing as well. Case in point; in America's classrooms today, teachers must reduce the use of countless dittos and meaningless worksheets. Instead, they could use more pen-pencil-paper technology with their students. Maybe teachers, parents, and students will discover what I have observed about today's youth. That is to say, children are writers too. And we need to teach them how to use and access information from the greatest and most available computer ever made—the human brain (10 billion cells of memory). Do you want young people to learn more about the BRAIN computer? Have them start sketching and writing. Teach school-age children how to use their fingers to write down information—on a blank sheet of paper—from a very powerful source with unlimited access and immeasurable software...the human brain.

According to Jean Piaget

And David Elkind,

INTELLIGENCE TESTS

only MEASURE…

CHILDREN LEARNING BEYOND
THE STANDARDIZED TEST

A procedure to determine a child's relative achievement level;
administered to a large group of children so that any one child's score
can be compared to the norm.
—Hallahan and Kauffman, *Exceptional Children*

During the early 1900s, American psychologist Lewis Terman presented educational research with a benchmark intelligence test (the Stanford-Binet) for the purpose of measuring learning in children. Since then, in the United States, various public-school districts and many private schools are continuing to use a combination of standardized tests to assess a child's attainment of formal knowledge— the Iowa Test of Basic Skills, the California Achievement Test, the School and College Ability Tests. As a point of reference, it is very common to read about school systems implementing curriculums and innovative programs to increase or improve students' achievement test scores. Some school districts and a number of parochial schools report, from time to time, that some children are showing cognitive gains in certain areas of these standardized tests. However, other children who annually take a battery of standardized achievement tests still have great difficulty producing acceptable test results.

Based upon my observations of standard educational practices during the last five years, there seems to be a growing number of educators, parents, and education practitioners who strongly feel that standardized testing alone does not and cannot truly measure accurately the vastness and depth of children's knowledge and their ability to learn. In numerous conversations I've had with parents, teachers, students, and supporters of educational values, they've all repeatedly expressed their dissatisfaction with the process and emphasis of standardized testing. And it's important to note, the pervasive educational method of using normative data continues to represent what Swiss psychologist Jean Piaget and American humanist David Elkind illustrated several years ago in their research related to the intellectual development of children. According to both Piaget and Elkind, intelligence tests only measure children's ability to give specific or correct answers to certain questions and do not measure or assess to any degree of consistency what children really know, nor the learners' level of thinking and readiness.[1] Furthermore, education researchers Walter R. Borg and Meredith D. Gall, in their 1989 book *Educational Research*, caution that many tests of intelligence often discriminate against minority children by way of cultural bias.

In addition, Borg and Gall point out the fact that these standardized tests are not always age-appropriate, and the statistical subscores could lack evidence of validity and/or reliability. These experts also report that the contents of many normative tests do not assess or collaborate with the subject matter or courses being taught in the schools. Borg and Gall conclude by stressing that the inconsistencies of administering the tests, misinterpreting test results, and public relations problems contribute to other mistakes involving standardized tests.

Therefore, school counselors, parents, classroom teachers, and school administrators must be careful when they interpret, post, discuss, and give feedback of test data. Children's confidentiality must be protected at all times. One should also compare a child's test subscores to his or her benchmark performance scores on previous tests. In this manner, a child's performance in testing is first compared to him/herself. Regarding the improvement of public relations within school districts, private schools, and municipalities, educators need to discontinue the practice of publishing schools' standardized test results, as they are sometimes printed in newspapers. In many cases when low scores are made public, some people form negative perceptions of education and lower their expectations of children. Instead, we must teach today's children how to learn by using their own innate abilities and talents.

Imperatively speaking, the process of teaching youngsters how to learn more effectively must include good parenting skills, effective teaching strategies, and efforts to develop in students a sincere appreciation for hard work. Thus, all youngsters will be nurtured through learning and continue progressive levels of attainment beyond testing. It's so true that if Pablo Picasso, the genius of painting and sculpture, were a modern-day American student, he probably would not pass any standardized tests—attitudinal scales, diagnostic tests, intelligence tests, achievement tests, aptitude tests, etc. Why? At times, Picasso could not remember or recall the alphabet.

Now the different test summations are ready for your analysis. And it is also time to do some powerful counseling and teaching by meeting the real challenge beyond testing...of preparing young people for life.

Finally, and with great respect, bravo and sincere accolades for those school systems and private education settings that have been able to successfully raise their pupils' standardized test scores while enhancing the achievement levels of students.

[1] R. Murray Thomas, *Comparing Theories of Child Development* (Belmont, California: Wadsworth Inc., 1985), p. 295.

LINES

for

SAVING   *our*

CHILDREN

THE YOUTH PHYSICAL
FITNESS DILEMMA

One problem in our technological society is that many American children ages 6 to 12 are not physically fit because they have not developed the necessary motivation for staying in shape. These young people lack the personal commitment necessary for maintaining and achieving acceptable levels of physical fitness.

The normative data presented by the University of Michigan Institute for Social Research indicate that a considerable number of elementary school children between the ages of 6 and 12 are not physically fit in the areas of cardiorespiratory endurance, muscular endurance, strength, and flexibility. Moreover, the President's Council on Physical Fitness maintains that American children are in bad shape physically because 40 percent of male students ages 6 to 12 can only do one pull-up, and one in four is unable to do any. Seventy percent of female students ages 6 to 12 complete only one pull-up while 55 percent fail in attempting to do so. In the fifty-yard dash, ten-year-old girls posted slower times than girls in the same age group ten years ago.

According to the U.S. Department of Health and Human Services, American children are facing increased health risks due to increased television watching and inactivity. This department reported that 40 percent of children ages 5 to 8 were showing evidence of major health risk factors associated with causing heart disease (high cholesterol, high blood pressure, sedentary lifestyle) and obesity in children. Regrettably, the results represent empirically a great need to seriously address the problem of our youths' physical fitness dilemma.

In retrospect, other related studies suggested that youth inactivity and excessive television viewing are causal factors in prohibiting acceptable physical fitness standards among certain children today. Unfortunately, school programs have not kept pace with the demands to counter the lackadaisical attitudes and negative perceptions about youth fitness.

For example, the *Journal of Sports Medicine* stated emphatically that the success of school programs has been impeded by financial restraints, the decline of overall academic performances among students, increased television viewing, and the perception that exercising and running are less pleasurable experiences. It remains increasingly doubtful that school programs will readjust to meet the very basic physical fitness requirements of youth. Therefore, practitioners must continue to synthesize solutions related to developing wellness attitudes in children by appropriately applying consistent teaching strategies and relevant program design concepts of learning. Recently, in a survey of 52 southeastern suburban seventh-grade students (*Clarifying and Communicating Values Through Physical Education and Sports Activities for Seventh Grade Students*), Singleton indicated that 20 respondents wanted additional help in establishing firm physical fitness goals and maintaining a healthier lifestyle.

The watershed effect of these factors touches upon extended school care for children, public education, human health versus sedentary living, the influence of television, and declines in the physical fitness of youth.

The immediate and long-term impact of youth inactivity and increased health risks strongly call for intervention on virtually every level from within the American society or human ecological system. The current American community is one in which cultural diversity, institutional conformity, domestic issues, communications systems, confutations, parental pressures, children's needs, individual differences, and international concerns present an array of crucial challenges for our youth.

Theoretically speaking, this present era has been called an age of science, an age of nostalgia, an age of international communication, an age of hope. Needless to say, it is all of these things and many other social variables as well.

In society, the family represents a key factor in preserving culture, humanity, and civilization. Hence, this present era is also an age of understanding the family. However, some households are chronically disadvantaged with various emotional and psychological dysfunctions. Consequently, many children are overstressed because their families do not know how to deal effectively with issues and demographic trends involving single parenting, latchkey children, violence, child abuse, poverty, multicultural education, technology, sedentary living, and out-of-shape children. Sad to say, as Americans continue to spend billions of dollars on today's sporting equipment, sportswear, and various sports fitness items, these children may or may not have a healthier future in the next century...let alone the coming millennium. Instead of our youth at this particular moment in human history acquiring a field of dreams, they could very well end their lives prematurely and rest forever in a field of tombstones.

Therefore, in order to reduce the number of sedentary-related illnesses, I strongly recommend that parents, educators, nutritionists, legislators, health-care professionals, and other advocates work together to promote longevity, happiness, and prosperity for people living today and the next generation of children.

Source

Singleton, C. L. *A Multiple Activities Program to Improve the Physical Fitness Performances of Fifth-Grade Students.* Unpublished manuscript, NOVA Southeastern University, Program in Child and Youth Studies. Fort Lauderdale, FL, 1993.

The

WELLNESS

CHALLENGE

THE SINGLETON MODIFIED ORIENTEERING TASKS

The goal of the Singleton Modified Orienteering Tasks is to improve the basic physical fitness skills of school-age children. The program is designed to include a combination of teacher-student selected physical education activities and other school-related subjects—reading, mathematics, science, music, and social studies.

Materials needed:
(3) Student dictionaries
(2) Magnetic compasses
(2) Stopwatches
(1) Globe
(1) 25-foot measuring tape
(3) Science books
(3) Social studies textbooks
Related background music

The Setting:
Indoor physical education

Task Items:
12 (1–3 students per task)

Completion Time:
20–30 minutes

Orienteering Tasks

During indoor physical education, have students select a particular activity assignment for improving physical fitness performances from the following list.

Task Numbers, Assignments, and Physical Fitness Outcomes

1. Walk to the media center and count the number of volumes in a set of encyclopedias. Return to class and repeat the answer by doing the same number of side straddle hops (heart and lung fitness).

2. Walk into the cafeteria and count the number of tables. Return to class and repeat the answer by doing the same number of side straddle hops OR jump and reach (heart and lung fitness).

3. Walk to the athletic "Wall of Achievement" and count the number of school records posted for track and field events. Return to class and do a series of warm-up and conditioning exercises for five to ten minutes (heart and lung fitness, flexibility, muscular strength, muscular endurance).

NOTE: Exercises could include deep breathing, body stretching, side straddle hops, alternate toe touches, windmills, jogging in place, push-ups, body balancing, pull-ups, sit and reach, and arm curls.

4. Take out your social studies book and read for five minutes. Explain to your classmates what you have just read through a series of body movements (wellness and physical fitness).

5. Using a magnetic compass, walk out the number of degrees (in steps) for a circle and right angle (wellness and physical fitness).

6. Using a magnetic compass, draw a map for walking to other classrooms and in the halls. Complete this assignment by walking through the pathway you have created (wellness and physical fitness).

7. Using a magnetic compass and aerobic walking, find the 32 points and use this information to locate 32 different objects in the classroom (wellness and physical fitness).

8. Using a tape measure or ruler, map out on the floor a standing long jump self-test. Measure each jump, then repeat the jump and try to increase your distance by 3 inches (muscular endurance).

9. Using a science book or dictionary, find the meanings of 10 different science words. Now do 10 exercises starting with the first letter of each word (wellness and physical fitness).

10. Using a globe, find 15 countries that you would like to visit someday. Now become a financial whiz-kid-globetrotter and walk out the amount of money in steps it would cost to visit 3 countries (walking wellness for life).

11. Using a stopwatch, time yourself before, during, and after the (indoor) aerobic walking. Try to increase your heart rate to 120–150 beats per minute (heart and lung fitness).

12. Cool down—stretch, relax, listen to music, read a book. Now aerobic-walk for 20 minutes (fitness for life).

SUCCESS

ACHIEVING AND MAINTAINING
SUCCESS

In my role as an education consultant/journalist, I am frequently asked to speak to groups of people about strategies for achieving their personal goals in life. Over the years, I have experienced and observed that successful individuals practice the dynamics of thinking throughout the day. By this I mean such thinkers actively turn their thoughts into positive energy and productivity. I have also noticed that successful people have a kind of soliloquy or mantra when talking to themselves. The following definitions and incantations for improving human performance are practiced continuously by high achievers.

- Personal success is the habitual moderation of one's attitudes toward life.
- Success comes with temperance (i.e., self-control, discipline).

Monday

To consistently achieve and maintain spiritual, physical, emotional, psychological, academic, and social success, do what is required and a little more every day. (In other words, overreach your daily goals.)

Tuesday

Save ten cents, one dollar, or ten dollars—the power of ten. DO NOT intoxicate yourself by overspending. Investing and saving money will help you to achieve and maintain a better standard of living.

Wednesday

Time, energy, and money. Everyone has the same amount of time: 60 seconds in a minute; 60 minutes in an hour; 24 hours in a day. Recently, a spacecraft reported that time started approximately 15 billion years ago (15,000,000,000). Time moves at the same pace. Time is conditional. Time is virtuosity. Time is passion for living and improving one's own lifestyle. Your personal or individual success depends on how you use time, energy, and money.

Thursday through Sunday

Patience. Patience is practice. Patience is a virtue. Patience is the habitual moderation of attitudes, appetites, and of your life's goals. We live in a society that says to us, "I wanted this on my desk yesterday! Fax it now! Why didn't you use the remote control?"

Come on, my friends; practice being patient. Remember, it takes 1 million years for a clump of sand to become a solitaire diamond and 30 years or more to grow a tree mature enough to be made into paper.

Finally, underachievers in the areas of talents, efforts, and life goals allow themselves to become impregnated with poisonous thoughts, gossip, idle talk, and newsmongering habits. They lack the virtue of patience. Our children must learn that life is measured by attainment, self-discipline, and a vision of a healthy existence.

Readers of this article must always remember to practice their faith and belief in a Supreme Being.

WITH PURPOSE

Forty years ago, in my hometown of Summerville, South Carolina, parents and patrons of Alston High School paid a tremendous price for public education and youth sports development. In return, the student population performed with distinction.

Dear old Alston High was small (600 students), segregated, and underfunded. The parade of hand-me-down books, buses, various band instruments, football pads, and unfulfilled promises were standard modes of school administration. Seemingly, larger quantities of current educational resources went to the school across town. Alston High, "Dear Ole Alston High," like so many Black schools of that era, had to always "make do."

This present era supposedly has been called an age of obvious prosperity for many African Americans. Some people even say, without a doubt, our entire educational process has uniquely upgraded itself since the post-war fifties and turbulent sixties. Therefore, we as a people in many cases don't have to "make do." Really? Yet, other individuals and pundits in our society make merry over tangible superficial quota. Still, there is another compendium or summary that keeps all of us in touch with those years of continual mock and pacification. Surely, the fifties and sixties have passed into history's graveyard. However, and sadly too, the problems of those periods are staying with society and touching us today.

For this reason, the Summerville-Black struggle for existence transcends the dormant seventies, uncertain eighties, and fearful nineties. Yes, "Ole Alston High, Dear Ole Alston," we truly loved you. For **you** the African-American community expressed its talents, aspirations, religion, academics, and sports. In return, the student population of that time performed with distinction. (By the way, this particular achievement was somewhat puzzling to the populace living on the other side of the railroad tracks. How did we achieve so much academically, musically, socially, culturally, economically, and athletically on meager contributions?). Black families were sending their children to colleges and various universities in record numbers. Our proud band, directed by Mr. Jones and Mr. Devore, played excerpts from Tchaikovsky, Beethoven, and Rossini's opera *William Tell.* The choir performed James Weldon Johnson's works to near perfection. Our little single-A school had to compete athletically against three AAA rivals because of gas allocation and distance. Nevertheless, the Tiger football club was a championship contender yearly. Small in size, big in heart, well-coached, and determined to win were all characteristics of the Alston High School football teams.

From time to time, we look back upon those days and ask, "How did we make over?" I am most certain that this question was on the agenda when the boys met at *The 5220 Club, Many Faces,* and *Clay Belle* around Christmastime. The *Duck Inn,* Robert Smalls, and Willie Thomas' *Do Drop Inn,* also carried their conversations back twenty, thirty, and maybe forty years to address the same question. Some of the old stars, latecomers, unsung heroes, and haven't seen yas, talked all night about how Alston defeated Burke, Bonds Wilson, and several other schools from Charleston in 1962. In retrospect, many locals acknowledged prayer, faith, and the "Never Say Die" attitude instilled by Coach Jimmy Greene as part of the reasons for Alston's athletic success.

We look back and see our hometown of the late '50s and '60s, with an average annual income of less than three thousand dollars per black family. For the most part we were farmers, pulpwood loggers, brick masons, carpenters, maids, and yard workers. Some fathers—and very few mothers—had jobs at the Charleston Air Force Base and naval port. It was common to see yard workers being paid fifty cents an hour. How then was it possible for Alston's band to get new uniforms, instruments, and music sheets? The football field got lights! The choir got robes! And how much did the local school board give us? Just for the record, I'll say very, very little compared to what was needed. The financial difference was made up by the bean pickers' extra fifty cents; or maybe finances were boosted by the cotton pickers who got three cents a pound for picking cotton. It very well could have been the church deacons, matrons, and mothers who prayed basically the same prayer every Sunday.

Bless our families, church,
homes, and community.

Help the school, football
team, and band. Help those
who are prison-bound.
Protect our loved ones on
yonder's battlefields.

I look back on those days with a sense of loss. Certainly, I wouldn't want to return to the segregated schools, low wages, the struggle for existence. Yet, I miss the tightly knit community that helped us transcend the obstacles. Where are the committed parents now who will make great sacrifices to improve their children's schools? In Summerville, South Carolina, we didn't have many opportunities, but our parents made sure we capitalized on the ones we had. We helped each other and, as a result, grew stronger and achieved more. Now, it is our turn to work together as adults to inspire and help young people.

We've gained material resources but lost our sense of community. We're also missing out on new opportunities. In my profession, sports education consultant, I see talented athlete after talented athlete channeled into the same sports—football, track and field, baseball, and basketball. Where are the African-American gymnasts and tennis players? Where are the hockey, swimming, figure skating, skiing, and golf stars? Perhaps the recent successes of golfer Tiger Woods and gymnast Dominique Dawes will continue to encourage other African-American youngsters to actively pursue their dreams in sports. Our children can learn the skills of golf and the compulsories of gymnastics; they can learn the delicate, crisp backhand volley in tennis. In order for them to excel in an individually oriented sport, they need our support.

Please remember, we must decide our true destiny in sports. For centuries past and even today, our role in all sports and games has been limited to being the player, rarely manager or coach, never owner. Up to this point in sports history, the real player (i.e., owner/investor) has undoubtedly shaped rules of play, not us. Henry Wadsworth Longfellow declared, "A person has two basic choices in a society. Shape society or be shaped by it." One way is through the creation of more opportunities for African-American children to participate in club sports (e.g., golf, tennis, gymnastics, hockey, swimming, figure skating, skiing). W.E.B. DuBois talked about developing the "Talented Tenth." On the other hand, Booker Taliaferro Washington reminded us to sometimes "cast down our buckets where we are." For the sake of not arguing their educational philosophies, try combining the three concepts. Perhaps you'll discover what I did.

It was the flag that inspired Francis Scott Key to write this country's national anthem. James Weldon Johnson's "Lift Every Voice and Sing" was inspired by his unfortunate experiences and quest for human dignity and equality. Once again become inspired and help youngsters develop their dreams. As Longfellow asked, "Anvil or hammer?" Which are you?

The Kitchen Table:
FOOD FOR THOUGHT

The lack of parent-child discussions about life may be one of the contributing factors to so many young people apparently developing serious behavioral problems in our society today. This writer may or may not have a valid point as he attempts to identify inappropriate actions expressed by our youth, but defiant, violent, disruptive, and disrespectful behaviors clearly indicate that something is missing in the home-training of these children.

As a public school teacher observing children in various social and educational settings, this writer sees many indications that children miss the experience of talking and/or communicating with parents and other adults. In the school lunchroom, for example, some children display poor choices in the foods they select, disregard the lunchroom rules, ignore discipline by teachers or other adults, use inappropriate language or loud voices and sometimes violent actions with their peers. In the classroom, many young children entering school are unable to express themselves or answer simple questions.

What has caused this recent change in our youth's behavior? In America today, millions of school-age children eat their meals away from parents, home, and the kitchen table. During school hours, it is common for students to eat both breakfast and lunch at school. Additionally, many latchkey children and adolescents eat alone or with other siblings during the dinner or supper hour. Finally, a quick stop at a local restaurant's drive-through window is quite common and becomes the kitchen table when younger children are picked up from day care centers and after-school programs in the late afternoons and early evenings.

Two generations of minors are the product of the influence and consumption of restaurants' fast foods. Very seldom is there face-to-face contact between adults and youth during the periods of automobile mealtime. Numerous parents, guardians, and protectors of children have spent countless hours talking to their loved ones from the front seats of cars. Usually, the children are seated in the back seats while food is passed to them.

A second scenario that illustrates interference of parent-child communications takes places when meals are eaten in front of the television. Everyone's attention is focused on television broadcasting rather than on sharing the day's events with each other.

A final cause occurs when it becomes necessary for parents to hold multiple jobs, thereby keeping the adults in the family away from the children.

Family talks about suitable and timely decision-making strategies are positive ingredients for any child's normal development. These talks and discussions can take place anywhere, usually around a kitchen table or at mealtimes. Talking and discussion helps prepare children for the world outside their homes. It teaches the children who they are in the grand scheme of things.

"Now, where are your manners?" one person may ask. They are

around and at the kitchen table. You see, this writer has observed that well-mannered and well-nurtured young individuals (i.e., homegrown) do become courteous adults. Seriously, family conversations at breakfast, lunch, and dinner have become a luxury of the past. Today's busy schedules and demands on parental time do not leave time for parents to eat a leisurely meal with their families.

Children need help clarifying confusing issues concerning day-to-day living. Needless to say, they are very much dependent on knowledgeable parents, guardians, and caregivers for leadership involving personal conflicts. Moment by moment, young people are faced with insurmountable decisions and unresolved feelings about family responsibilities, peer acceptance, social roles, and various psychological concerns including sexual identity, self-esteem, fear, guilt, withdrawal, depression, and helplessness. These psychosocial characteristics are a part of early childhood, adolescence, and young adulthood. Young individuals need help overcoming these unresolved issues as they move into adulthood.

What solutions can be implemented to solve some of these problems? In order to stem the tide of young fellows engaging in unacceptable and inappropriate behavioral patterns, grown-ups need to take an about-face and a change of attitude by using the old family circle—the kitchen table. When a fast-food meal is the only choice, stop for a short time, go inside the restaurant, and eat with the children at a table. The time taken will do wonders for our youth while giving grown-ups time to relax. If the family has taken time to go on a picnic, to a movie, or to a local attraction, parents can help children learn to express themselves by asking questions about the event while riding in the car on the way home. An effective parent asking questions like, "What did you like best about the movie?" or, "Who was your favorite character in the story?" assures the child that his/her opinions are valid, and that they count. In a restaurant, children should be given one or two choices about what to order. This teaches children how to select nutritional foods for maintaining a balanced diet. At all times, children should be taught to share a variety of thoughts about daily experiences with other family members. Moreover, this particular opportunity of sharing ideas conversationally gives each person a turn to talk.

This writer strongly believes that all parents strive to be responsible parents. Heads of households, parents, guardians, and caregivers must do more toward properly training their children at home! Maybe, if the kitchen table were used to assure more quality time within families, many young people could avoid becoming casualties of underachievement and disgrace. We must remember constantly that children are gifts to the world and our greatest resource for replicating man's existence and improving his future.

Without a doubt, the kitchen table conferences with family members during mealtimes do symbolize a healthier lifestyle that teaches and nurtures, not only acceptable table manners, but social skills for a productive life as well. This writer, parent, and educator strongly feels that the kitchen table approach to involving parents and children in active talking and listening (face-to-face) will produce the following outcomes:

- Children and adolescents who have respect and consideration for the rights of others.
- Children and adolescents who have a better understanding of societal rules and personal responsibilities.
- Children and adolescents who recognize and value the importance of staying in school and obtaining a good education.

All youth will have opportunities to discuss and clarify values associated with personal goals, sexual identity, success, failure, recognition, health, physical fitness, appearance, motivation, achievement, honesty, religion, and citizenship.

The challenge, therefore, is to provide numerous possibilities for youngsters to think, grow, feel, and use their own judgment about the nature of being human.

Education: TEACHERS NEED MORE LETTERS OF SUPPORT

B ack in November 1996, I received the following letter of gratitude from a parent whose children attended Edward L. Bouie, Sr. Elementary Traditional Theme School in DeKalb County, Georgia.

> *11/6/96*
>
> *Dear Coach Singleton,*
>
> *Thanks for teaching my daughter Ashlee the Heimlich Maneuver. I believe it saved my younger daughter Candace's life.*
>
> *While at home after school, Candace choked on a sandwich and fell to the floor. By using her quick action, Ashlee, the older sister, was able to remember the maneuver, and use it effectively to help her sister. Candace is fine now! Also, thanks for taking the time to teach CPR to the students, and giving them the confidence to use it in times of need.*
>
> *Forever Grateful*
>
> *Betty Lee*

Needless to say, I was emotionally overwhelmed with compassion and contentment after learning about a child's life being saved following the appropriate first-aid action of her older sibling. For my colleagues and me, Ms. Betty Lee's complimentary letter succinctly created an impressionable and indelible moment for the teachers and educators. The emotional and psychological impact of Ms. Lee's correspondence greatly improved our faculty's morale and esprit de corps. Professionally, we are still invigorated by the thoughts of this positive outcome.

Granted, in such an emergency, Ashlee's knowledge of the highly effective Heimlich Maneuver proved to be an invaluable lifesaving skill. American Surgeon H. J. Heimlich developed and first used this technique for dislodging food from the throat of a person who is choking. Noteworthy: At Edward L. Bouie, Sr. Elementary Traditional Theme School, physical educators Ms. Doris Woodruff-Jackson and Dr. Charles L. Singleton have successfully taught both the Heimlich Maneuver and Cardiopulmonary Resuscitation (CPR) as an intrinsic entity of Theme School Education.

In summation, I would like to suggest that both disgruntled parents—and parents who are satisfied with public education—write more letters of support to teachers and educators. According to Anne Henderson, author of *The Evidence Continues to Grow: Parent Involvement Improves Student Achievement,* students whose parents effectively communicate with their teachers simply perform better in school and throughout life.

Public School Education: WHERE DO WE GO FROM HERE?

In the 1500s, according to an encyclopedic review of educational science, Polish astronomer Nicholas Copernicus predicted that Earth was not the center of the universe. Instead, Copernicus postured that the sun was at the very center of the planetary system. In postulating his heliocentric viewpoint, Nicholas Copernicus rattled the human psyche with this piercing notion of Earth's relative position in the solar system.

In a like manner, author John Holt's 1964 publication *How Children Fail* caused educators and the lay public to rethink educational goals and practices.

Holt's observations suggested that in many of America's public schools, the art of effective teaching and progressive learning in children was nil or nonexistent. Holt maintained that creative abilities in children were being thwarted by very dull and meaningless instructional tasks. And because some children were totally disinterested in completing the inordinate amount of teacher-directed assignments, their innate desires for knowledge were squelched (i.e., repetitive work in the classroom which required limited usage of the brain to successfully solve a problem or to provide an academic challenge). According to John Holt, the instructional climate described above greatly impedes learning in young people. Therefore, this contradistinction, observed by Holt, could be one of the main reasons why a varying number of students fail to achieve and maintain academic proficiency in public schools today.

The solution to improving education for all children lies in part with parents maintaining constructive support for their children, teachers, and schools during twelve years of schooling. In addition, today's universities and colleges must focus more energy toward developing a humanistic approach in education, and also train future teachers and administrators in how to better teach and manage children who come from varied cultures and different socioeconomic backgrounds. Meanwhile, staff development courses for experienced educators must be taught in conjunction with the same humanistic objectives implemented by teacher-training programs in higher education. All educators must become more proficient in the art of classroom management, human tolerance and understanding, collaborative education, and facilitative learning.

Ms. Joyce Walthour, a high school science teacher in Atlanta, Georgia, experienced that creativity in the learner is strongly enhanced when the teacher serves as a facilitator. Also, this array of educational methods would be strengthened through what researcher Daniel Goleman calls "emotional intelligence." Goleman believes that children who acquire experiential knowledge through the applications of emotional intelligence will become progressive learners throughout life.

Finally, I do agree that the litany of societal problems which negatively affect students' learning will continue to discourage some education practitioners. However, the question still remains—as a literacy-based society, where do we go from here? Do education professionals continue the arduous day-to-day practice of inundating teachers and administrators with endless monitory duties, relentless responsibilities, monumental and legal accountability, and a paper trail of various reports? Painstaking as it seems, the modern teaching profession will have to create a suitable pathway for educating all children, regardless of their ethnicity and socioeconomic backgrounds. We must not *under-educate* the resourceful minds of the next century. Educational experiences of young learners will have to exceed their abilities to regurgitate only classroom knowledge if they are to become productive adults. EUREKA! Now, where do we go from here?

December 31, 1999

11:59 PM

The National Education Goals:
TIME IS RUNNING OUT!

In 1990, education reform was on the agendas of politicians, educators, parents, and advocates for lifelong learning. As a matter of fact, on January 21, 1990, President George H. W. Bush introduced six national education goals in his State of the Union Address, which were to serve as guidelines and objectives for improving schools and the education of children and adults.

The National Goals for Education presented by President George Bush were the following:

Goal 1: Readiness for School—By the year 2000, all children in America will start school ready to learn.

Goal 2: High School Completion—By the year 2000, the high school graduation rate will increase to at least 90 percent.

Goal 3: Student Achievement and Citizenship—By the year 2000, American students will leave grades four, eight, and twelve having demonstrated competency in challenging subject matter including English, mathematics, science, history, and geography; and every school in America will ensure that all students learn to use their minds well, so they may be prepared for responsible citizenship, further learning, and productive employment in our modern economy.

Goal 4: Science and Mathematics—By the year 2000, US students will be first in the world in science and mathematics achievement.

Goal 5: Adult Literacy and Lifelong Learning—By the year 2000, every adult American will be literate and will possess the knowledge and skills necessary to compete in a global economy and exercise the rights and responsibilities of citizenship.

Goal 6: Safe, Disciplined, and Drug-Free Schools—By the year 2000, every school in America will be free of drugs and violence and will offer a disciplined environment conductive to learning.

On February 1, 1991, President George H. W. Bush wrote a letter to the governors of the United States with the hope of establishing a workable education plan to improve education for the nation. President Bush's ebullient strategy to enhance the national goals for education was to form a "federal-state partnership" for the 1990s and the year 2000. The nation has only a few months left before the end comes to this decade. A decade still characterized by students who underachieve in our schools and society, as seen in the pervasive increase of school suspensions, dropouts, violence, drugs, tardiness, and illiteracy. Also, various research reports continue to remind us about the millions of school-age children who will be unprepared for school because of child abuse, parental neglect, and exposure to crack cocaine.

We are very close to the countdown for the year 1999. The time has truly come for politicians, educators, parents, and advocates for lifelong learning to assess the 1990 National Goals for Education. After your assessment of today's educational progress, standards, improvements, and deficiencies, please work toward helping children and adults improve their abilities to learn. Moreover, the nation's governors, education enthusiasts, and President Bill Clinton must continue to review and assess the education policies and initiatives presented at the 1989 Education Summit held in Charlottesville, Virginia.

Source

The National Educational Goals: A Second Report to the Nation's Governors. Available from the White House, Office of the Press Secretary, Washington, D.C., February 1991.

AND THAT IS WHAT RAP MUSIC
IS ALL ABOUT

Whether you like the poetic words or not, the lyric utterances of rap and its musical accompaniment are here to stay for a while. Why? Because ever since the creation of mankind, special words, rhythms, or sounds have been used by human beings to express a particular emotion or to name a person, place, or thing. It is safe to say that all languages have a name for the sun, moon, stars, and water. It is also fair to assume that all languages have a traditional statement, phrase, or vernacular for telling an acquaintance goodbye (arrivederci, au revoir, adios, auf wiedersehn, etc.). In like manner, the so-called lyricists of rap are not only saying their goodbyes, but more importantly, they are speaking to those of us who are willing to listen. Hello! Are you there? The persnickety melodies of rap music are pervasive tones of Homo Sapiens!

Yes! "We, the young hopefuls of this era have something to tell you; will you listen?" Maybe in this modern age of computers, answering machines, e-mail, beepers, and cellphones, our youths are trying to tell other humans that they need to have a talk. Educator and child-care professional Deborah Walker-Little of Norcross, Georgia, concluded that "a person who raps is telling his or her own story and hoping frantically that other people are listening." Frankly, the task of finding a clear and concise explanation for rap is as elusive as its actual origin. The audiences of popular music believe that either rap has no generic beginning or that rap music is a derived entity, entwined with other musical compilations—karaoke, calypso, rock 'n' roll, rhythm and blues, pop, hip-hop, country, rock, reggae, soul, jazz, musical slang, etc.

However, the comments about this repetitive juggernaut do not stop with an empirical investigation into the emergence of rapping. According to teenager Khristopher Miller, a junior at Cedar Grove High School in Ellenwood, Georgia, "listening to rap music is the in thing to do for some people." Khris, who is one of Cedar Grove High School's drum majors, summarizes that young people listen to rap because they like to hear the rant of rhythmical beats, rhyming lyrics, and music to dance by. Khristopher Miller, along with other members of this young generation, said that high school teens listen to rappers because of peer pressure and the absence of parental communication.

Another observation of this style and type of popular music is the vocalists' usage of repugnant speech during a song. Such horrid renditions often appeal to a number of listeners. However, many rap enthusiasts would rather hear musical compositions without profanity and vulgarity. Now you know, and that is what rap music is all about.

Adults and parents, please try to listen and communicate with society's greatest resource—our children; your sons and daughters. Besides, the day of reckoning is certainly upon us. Truly, the rapid calls and responses of this raspy-loquacious repertoire must be answered by all individuals, especially parents. I *willkommen* you to the intractable world of adolescence.

SIMPLE SOLUTIONS

Probably, during ancient times, prehistoric women and men solved the various problems they faced by using simple solutions. For example, to keep a boat or ship from going adrift or out to sea, the ancients invented and used anchors to keep these vessels fixed in a particular place. Another primal device used by people who lived during earlier moments of human history was the ax. The powerful ax, a crude, man-made tool used primarily for cutting wood, has helped mankind to build houses, roads, ships, bridges, and monuments. The third problem-solver of past civilizations was the invention called writing. The person who actually created writing is unknown. Retrospectively, lexicographers, calligraphers, and scholars view writing or penmanship as the most important process for recording information. The inventiveness of humans allowed the creation of anchors, axes, and symbols for writing simple solutions.

Today, and as we progress toward the twenty-first century, we are faced with insurmountable problems ranging from A to Z. However, I am convinced that many of these seemingly unbearable difficulties are solvable. Now, readers, are you ready for my suggestions for improving human life on Earth? The simple solution for helping us to live better lives is called the do-it-yourselfer; and it is an invention that is available to everyone (initiator, originator, discoverer, planner, etc.) and you.

The next time you see an unsightly piece of paper or debris sprawling across your pathway, please reach down and try to safely remove it from the ground or surface. And on Sunday, when you go to church, if the hinges on the doors of this building are repeatedly making squeaky sounds with intolerable echoes, use your hands to fix them or create means to get the problem corrected. In other words, you must think symbolically of the historical significance involving the usage of anchors, axes, and writing. By acting as anchors in various organizations, you, readers, will prevent those communal systems from drifting into extinction. For those of you who have the broadax mentality, keep up the good work wherever you are and continue to be a battleax for correctness and humanity. Needless to say, "The pen is mightier than the sword." Ever since women and men have been able to write (8,000 years ago, a scholarly estimate), an incalculable number of man-made achievements have been recorded and improved.

Remember, do-it-yourselfers; both Alexander Graham Bell and George Washington Carver were discoverers who made things better for those of us who are living today. As a matter of fact, Alexander Graham Bell wanted to find a way to help young people who had impaired hearing. Graham Bell, through his attempts to find out the causes of deafness, made an amazing discovery—the telephone. In the same light, George Washington Carver, an American agricultural chemist, discovered ingenious ways to use the potato, soybean, peanut, and cotton for the production of many food and commercial products, such as cheese, soap, ink, and wood paints. Carver, a do-it-yourselfer, did more with a single peanut than Michael Jordon could ever do with a basketball. Get the message?

Yes, I agree emphatically that the problems of today appear to be overwhelming indeed (cancer, heart disease, abuse, suicide, Acquired Immune Deficiency Syndrome (AIDS), violence, crime, homelessness, overeating, parental absenteeism, poverty, ignorance, loss of imagination). One solution is the implementation of prevention and self-action. We must start practicing those positive behaviors which will reduce our risk of becoming victimized by some of these incurable nemeses. Everyone needs to research his or her life and really determine simple solutions for promoting better health and a brighter future. Hopefully, my friends, the next time and in this regard, journalistic cajolery will not be necessary to energize you. Arrivederci!

Just Think...

ALBERT EINSTEIN

CHILDREM ARE LEARNERS: NOT LABELS

It is ironic that in today's American society, where many more minority children are now attending public schools, school districts continue the irresponsible practice of labeling students with inappropriate names—slow learners, attention deficit disordered children, D students, culturally disadvantaged children, chronically challenged pupils, behaviorally deficient youngsters, difficult learners, hyperactive children, dysfunctional learners, standardized test failures, at-risk children…an endangered species. For example, the controversial label "attention deficit disorder" is often used by many psychiatric and education professionals to describe America's children who appear to have attentional problems. On Wednesday, December 11, 1996, Marilyn Elias in *USA Today* ("Ritalin use up among youth") reported that there is a considerable increase in the number of children and teenagers being placed on the drug Ritalin to treat their inattentiveness and perceptual hyperactivity. "The number of U. S. children and teens taking Ritalin for Attention Deficit Disorder (ADD) more than doubled between 1990 and 1995." According to Elias's article, researcher Daniel Safer of Johns Hopkins University Medical School found approximately 1.5 million people under the age of nineteen are using Ritalin. In their 1988 book *Exceptional Children,* Daniel P. Hallahan and James M. Kauffman conclude that the use and misuse of such psychostimulants (Ritalin, Dexedrine, Cylert) could even impede the learning process in some children during the formative years, while lowering teacher expectations

54

and fostering unresolved feelings of insecurity on the part of the learner. Needless to say, such stereotyped short phrases used to describe school-age children are both counterproductive and inharmonious to learning.

Readers and ardent supporters of children must stop this revolving door of education mediocrity with regard to labeling children and their ability to learn. The plethora of indifference, coupled with the potential psychological damage done to children by so-called educators, pseudointellectuals, and burdensome parents or guardians, might forever prevent these children from successfully entering the shopping mall of learning and its multiple aspects of knowledge. Therefore, adults must make a conscientious effort to stop calling children incorrigible names which could leave indelible, lifelong scars on their blossoming self-esteems.

It can be argued that the solution to this misperception of labeling school-age children must involve the retraining of classroom teachers, specialists, school administrators, as well as curriculum developers. Such retraining programs would include the science of pedagogy (methods of teaching). Parents and guardians would also need to spend more quality time with their children. In studies cited by The Young and Rubicam Foundation *(The One Place, 1991)*, a child's ability to learn greatly improves when the school protects the child and ensures the psychological, physical, and emotional development of the learner. Young and Rubicam further recommend that both parents and teachers must continually communicate high expectations in order for children to learn acceptable behaviors. And by doing so, maybe the perception of these negligent actions or behaviors involving some youth today in the United States will be eliminated. Therefore, the need to label children will be significantly reduced. Children are learners...not just labels.

Just think, Albert Einstein, the German-American physicist, was labeled a poor student, and his school performance was evaluated as substandard. If Albert Einstein were a student in one of our public schools today, he would surely be labeled a slow learner. Most likely, Einstein would also face a process of endless referrals amid the strident chorus of education practitioners. Children are learners...period.

A

PSYCHOLOGICAL

Journey

The Library: A GOOD PLACE FOR CHILDREN TO MENTALLY VIDEOTAPE

The library, public or private, remains an effective resource that could improve children's knowledge and lives. Yes, young people can truly save time, energy, and money by investing in the habit of taking intelligent footsteps through the historical annals and encyclopedic volumes of human history. Needless to say, there are literally countless numbers of written reports, wonderful stories, and astonishing events just waiting to be discovered by the young minds of children.

Believe it or not, a well-planned trip to the local or school library could take children and their curiosities through the ancient writings of the Egyptians, Chinese, Africans, and Greeks. During the same visit, children could take a mental flight to many other geographical places without purchasing an expensive airline ticket or entering a bus terminal. For example, a simple word search involving a family of words could possibly take voracious readers around the world. On this psychological journey, children would experience the continental surfaces that help to make up Earth's land masses. These youthful minds will be tested on the various languages spoken by the people of Africa, Asia, Antarctica, Australia, South America, Europe, and North America. Note: Antarctica does not have an indigenous population—only visiting scientists and other research groups.

Furthermore, the library continues to offer both factual and fascinating information about the most incredible computer ever made...the human body. And, if children are computer illiterate, do not worry! In libraries and media centers, dictionaries, encyclopedias, and volumes of reference works will help young people to learn about the human body. By the way, the human body has billions of cells with a different theme or learning resource for each unit of living matter; it's an amazing universe all by itself. Media specialists Ruth Johnson and Wanda Willcoxen of Edward L. Bouie, Sr. Elementary Traditional Theme School in DeKalb enhance their ability to learn by mentally traveling through the innumerable media resources (i.e., books, online computers, films, videotapes, microfiche, etc.).

Therefore, parents, the next time your children ask to rent a videocassette or attend a movie theater, take them to the most cost-effective video store in town, the library. The money you and your children will save could be reinvested for other more meaningful endeavors.

Clarifying and Communicating
Values Through Sports:
PERCEPTIONS OF ADOLESCENCE
AND SPORTS

S EEMINGLY, ever since Granville Stanley Hall, an American
psychologist and educator, published seminal theories about
adolescence in 1904, twentieth century education theorists have tried to
explain how teenagers grow and develop. Education researchers
generally believe that the onset of puberty helps to set the foundation for
continued human growth and development. More precisely, Swiss
psychologist Jean Piaget maintains that the formal operational stage of
human development exists in adolescents approximately eleven years of
age and older. During this period of human growth, young adolescents
develop the ability to use abstract information and logic when analyzing
hypothetical situations. They learn how to understand laws of
probability while developing their abilities to integrate, combine, and
use different types of information in problem-solving. The stage of
formal operational thinking comes into existence only if all other mental
structures have been established. A brain-damaged adolescent, for
example, may have difficulty constructing formal ideas and rational
thought.

As a result of intellectual growth, the adolescent is confronted with
several issues related to morality. With the adolescent's ability to use
abstract thought, he or she is able to judge values, morals, and other

social concerns. According to humanist Lawrence Kohlberg, the adolescent's integration into society starts with socialization. The adolescent learns to internalize family expectations, customs, and norms of a certain society. How well an adolescent adapts to society depends greatly on his/her moral judgments.

Kohlberg's three moral developmental levels are Premoral, Conventional, and Self-Accepted. At the Premoral level, children ten years of age and under conform to society's rules of right and wrong. The behaviors of these children are based on their internal perceptions of hedonistic consequences involving pleasure, punishment, rewards, and power. In the Conventional morality stage, adolescents follow and conform to the social order and expectations of the family and society. Adolescents learn the value of maintaining good relations, and what it means to be good boys and girls. Adolescents also learn the value of having self-approval and the approval of others. During the Self-Accepted phase of pubescence, older adolescents are confronted with values involving individual rights and universal ethics. In other words, adolescents' moral judgments are based on how they internalize individual and universal human rights.

Other researchers see parental influence on adolescents' ethics as being essential to the development of appropriate values, beliefs, and goals. Many child-development theorists indicate that some adolescents tend to adopt the very same values, beliefs, and goals as their parents.

Research also interconnects family, school, and other environmental

factors that impact adolescents' behavior; for example: influence regarding peers, overstressed families, victims of abuse, neglect, exclusion, and other cultural traumas. In many occurrences, the home environment is reflected in adolescents' behaviors.

In like manner, sports theorists believe that athletics, games, and competition create excellent conduits for learning personal values and improving attitudes. In contrast, some educators feel strongly that in America, many athletic programs place too much emphasis on winning, rather than on the values of participation alone. Still, many researchers state that it is unclear how appropriate values, morals, and attitudes are transmitted to adolescents during physical activities and games. It's important to note: during discussions with younger teenage athletes, the majority of them say that they already have good acceptable attitudes about sports, education, careers, and life.

In the meantime, the sports saga involving millions of adolescents is being played out competitively in the various athletic arenas of America's landscape today. One perplexity is the fact that we really do not know the messages being sent from one youth to another; nor do we, as participants and observers, truly understand what values are actually being learned by this highly active and youthful group (ages 11–18). For many adolescents, various sports activities and social interactions very seldom guarantee or assure the acquirement of moral values.

Frequently, this writer has observed that many teenagers express confusion in their roles of becoming mature adults and acceptable members of society. Collectively, my observations reveal that most youngsters want to behave appropriately and gain adult approval and peer acceptance. These vigorous individuals also consume or spend a great deal of time discussing issues pertaining to respect for authority, personal achievement, music, sexual identity, appearance, and sportsmanship.

Additional observations of adolescents' behaviors further indicate that some young people exhibit disciplinary problems—cheating, name-calling, fighting, improper value judgments, etc. Simply stated, many adolescents do not know how to deal effectively with moral issues and value judgments; nor do they seriously understand the role that sports activities play in communicating values.

Interestingly, it was not very long ago that I had the opportunity to watch a young man who appeared to be going through a terrible crisis. Seemingly, as it was, this particular person could not figure out the predicament or crisscross entanglement he was experiencing. In his selective soliloquy, he asked the question, "Why me?"

This juvenile never mentioned to me directly what was going on in his inner and social worlds. However, I could tell by his body language, during a solitary basketball practice, that he was obviously facing very unpleasant circumstances. Carefully, after a brief glance at his face and a little eye-to-eye contact, the puzzled-faced basketball player looked up and verbally acknowledged my presence. Suddenly, I inadvertently said,

"Say, tall man, I like your Yale University sweatshirt. Do you play basketball for Yale?"

With a look of bewilderment, he said, "No, and I don't know anything about that place." Later in the conversation, the youth implied that he had no intention of going to Yale or attending any school of higher learning, for that matter. He only bought the sweatshirt because it was an attractive shirt (matching colors, logo). Discouraging? Yes. Apparently, this student was "all dressed up with nowhere to go."

For some reason, this brief social encounter with the young high school student left me bespattered with the notion that he needed to desperately clarify values about his livelihood and future. Unfortunately, this paradoxical attitude of adolescent youth is pervasive throughout society today, as seen in the wearing of sports apparel (expensive shoes, clothing, garments) without an educational or physical fitness goal in mind. "Reach One, Teach One" helps an individual to set constructive goals in life and must be applied to help those such as the young athletic phenomenon described above.

Finally, these observations further imply that educators, coaches, and parents must continue to play an influential role in shaping teenagers' values, beliefs, and perceptions. In many cases, the best agents or examples for this process are responsive and interactive adults.

We all must allow adolescents many avenues to develop good peer relationships, individual identity, and educational goals. Teenagers typically exemplify what they already believe about human behavior and social expectations. The challenge, therefore, is to provide the navigable channels for adolescents to think, grow, feel, and to use their own judgment about sports activities, health, education, and life.

Source

Singleton, C. L. *Clarifying and Communicating Values Through Physical Education and Sports Activities for Seventh-Grade Students.* Unpublished manuscript, Nova Southeastern University, Program in Child and Youth Studies. Fort Lauderdale, FL, 1991.

References

Hall, G. S. *Adolescence.* New York: Appleton-Century-Crofts, 1904.

Kohlberg, L. *Essays on Moral Development.* Vol 2. New York: Harper and Row, 1984.

Piaget, J. *The Origins of Intelligence in Children.* New York: Norton, 1952.

BETWEEN...

Provocative

ESSAYS

Ebonics: A PATHWAY OR A DETOUR TO LEARNING?

Generally, all languages that are spoken by the peoples of various cultures represent simulative methods of communication. By speaking or using language, human beings can learn important knowledge about themselves and the world in which they live. In this same explanation of speech or language, dialects very often illustrate the many variations of particular patterns of verbal expressions within a language. Linguistically speaking, the similarities and differences between the words spoken or used by the peoples of the world serve only to distinguish the innumerable ways we express our emotions, demonstrate mental abilities, and utilize descriptive and complex utterances. Therefore, and in this frame of reference, some linguists, other citizens, and members of the Oakland, California, school board currently see Ebonics, African-American Vernacular English (AAVE), or Black English as an influential form of the English language.

Historically speaking, Czechoslovakian John Amos Comenius (1592–1670) advocated educating the school-age children of Moravia by teaching them in their everyday tongue, rather than in the language of Latin. Comenius strongly supported the theory that the conversational method involving the schooling of children in their own vernacular would also improve their potential to learn. However, it remains unclear how the Oakland, California, school board plans to implement a systemic-instructional approach for using Ebonics to enhance the academic performance of their students. According to Jacquelyn Cooper, a former Illinois Bell (Ameritech) communications and marketing expert in Chicago, "The Oakland, California, school superintendent and the school board are going to have a difficult time explaining to the lay public how the teaching of Ebonics or Black English will positively affect pupils' scholarly achievements; and the transference of idioms to standard English." And in Decatur, Georgia, Wendell White, a master barber (Upsweep Salon), prefers the teaching of standard English in schools over Ebonics for increasing opportunities for young people to learn and interpret modern information.

In order to become more employable in our highly technological society, African-American pupils and all school-age students will have to master standard English. In the twentieth century, as we continue to experience the infusing of languages and participate in a communicative global economy, both technological lingo (i.e., syntax, semantics) and standard English will have to be perfected by progressive users of contemporary speech. Examples of Americans who have successfully used the English language to inform mankind and to educate all Americans are as follows:

- Frederick Douglass (1817–1895): a self-educated orator and editor who wrote speeches brilliantly and spoke fluently about the plight and dilemma of African Americans during a most critical period in United States history.
- Barbara Jordan (1936–1996): an articulate Texas educator and eloquent public speaker who was elected to the United States House of Representatives in 1972.
- Mychal Wynn: raised in Chicago's South Side, graduated cum laude from Boston's Northeastern University and is the author of *Empowering African-American Males to Succeed*.
- Oprah Winfrey: host of a nationally syndicated weekday talk show and proprietor of Harpo Studio, Inc.

Readers, my genuine concern for presenting the viewpoints discussed above lies with the fact that we, as responsible adults, must objectively and critically analyze the true importance of maintaining impeccable and progressive standards in education today. Thomas Armstrong, in *Seven Kinds of Smart* (1993), states that learned individuals who have "linguistic intelligence" are "masters of literacy."

Thereupon, as an educator and essayist, I emphatically recommend to you the availability of the dictionary and substantial parental involvement as constructive pathways for improving pupils' learning. Just imagine. If the Oakland, California, school board and school boards across America would encourage or require every student enrolled in school to actually own, read, and use a dictionary to correct verbal mistakes and grammatical errors in their written and oral exercises, there would be very little need to teach some of America's children in Ebonics. Moreover, and greatly emphasized, parents who actively and constructively participate in their children's education help significantly improve these learners' academic performances and accomplishments. Ann Henderson, author of *The Evidence Continues to Grow: Parent Involvement Improves School Achievement*, reports the previously mentioned observation.

Finally, in the words of Danish physicist Niels Henrik David Bohr (1885–1962), "There are trivial truths and the great truths. The opposite of a trivial truth is plainly false. The opposite of a great truth is also true." (*Readers Digest,* July 1996, p. 124). Now, readers, do you think that Ebonics instruction is a navigable truth or a trivial truth for the enhancement of formal learning? Your children are learning and speaking which language? Hereunto, you must read between the lines instead of taking an abrupt detour to gaining knowledge. Obviously, in our sophisticated and technologically based culture of mass communication, global travel, artificial intelligence, facsimiles, factoids, and derivatives, our children are in desperate need of a dialectic education as opposed to dialectal schooling. A case in point: various research reports clearly indicate that immigrants entering the United States are currently taking standard English courses in record numbers.

Truly

A MYSTERY

Child Development: HOW DO CHILDREN LEARN ABOUT THEIR WORLD AND THEMSELVES?

B elieve it or not, the questions of how today's children actually learn about the art of living remains a puzzlement for parents and educators alike. This age-old interest has the adults in our technological society in a state of utter confusion. Seemingly, an individual would think that with all of the advancements in the world today, children's learning would be understood by parents, guardians, teachers, and significant others. Sadly, for many grown-ups, the knowledge of how youngsters acquire lifelong skills is truly a mystery. Well now. How do we humans learn?

Theoretically speaking, over the centuries, very thoughtful and brilliant minds have speculated over various ways in which children learn, grow, and develop. For instance, Greek philosophers Socrates (469–399 BC), Plato (428–347 BC), and Aristotle (384–322 BC) believed that the mind and the body were inseparable and that one's mental capacity to learn was enhanced through the attainment of self-knowledge. Socrates, in his discussions about human intelligence, maintained that clarity of information and rational thinking helped to create the impetus to learn. In addition, Plato, a student-disciple of Socrates, insisted that human thoughts, individual spirituality, and the universe were interconnected and also essential to learning. Plato, in his dialogues, further suggested that a person's ability to learn was refined by developing an inquiring mind. To complete the triumvirate of these earliest philosophic viewpoints, Aristotle concluded that both the manifestation and the application of logic were necessary in promoting learning. These most crucial assumptions (Socratic questioning, Platonistic-dialectic discussions, Aristotelian syllogism) shared by this trilogy of theorists offer paradigms for understanding how children learn about themselves and their surroundings.

Moreover, the birth, life, and death of Jesus Christ (approximately 2,000 years ago), whom many theologians call the world's greatest Teacher, exemplified and strengthened the fact that learning involves one's own faith, beliefs, positiveness, and a sense of universality. According to the Czechoslovakian education reformer John Amos Comenius (1592–1670), religion and science were harmoniously linked to the everyday experiences of the learner. Thus, a learner routinely obtains knowledge throughout his or her life by interacting with environmental dimensions and circumstances. English philosopher John Locke (1632–1704) strongly believed that a child's mind was like a blank sheet of paper, "tabula rasa," and served as a recorder for organizing life's experiences. Yet another theorist, Frenchman Jean Jacques Rousseau (1712–1778), emphasized that the influence of natural development was the most compelling ingredient in human learning. In other words, the interplay of the environment on youngsters' innate potentials greatly affects their natural growth and development. Simultaneously, during this period of history and philosophical posturing, Phillis Wheatley (1753–1784), a young American prodigy, was writing poetry at age fourteen that would have made the triumvirate of Greek philosophers very proud. Phillis Wheatley was an astute poetess and influential learner.

In the centennial years following Wheatley's poems and essays, evolutionist Charles Darwin (1809–1882) advocated that learning in human beings was a determinant based upon a series of genetic principles. Darwin inferred that heredity sets the stage and parameters for the acquirement of knowledge and the adaptations cited in his theory of evolution. More specifically, in the twentieth century, other philosophers have demonstrated that there are innumerable descriptive examples for understanding and suggesting how youngsters learn. The following list of theorists displays the varying pathways for learning.

- Charles Darwin (evolutionist): ethology and observable behavior
- John Dewey (experimentalist): personal experience and doable learning
- The Gestalt School (holists): integrated learning
- Sigmund Freud (psychoanalyst): satisfying the id, ego, and superego
- G. Stanley Hall (psychologist): learning to grow
- Ivan Pavlon (behaviorist): stimuli equal responses
- Jean Piaget (psychologist): cognitive learning, language skills, schemes, assimilation and accommodation
- Erik Erikson (psychoanalyst): personality and expectations

- Jerome Kagan (psychoanalyst): personality and learning
- George Washington Carver (scientist/educator): nature and knowledge
- Maria Montessori (educator): discovery, free-movement activities, the five senses, self-motivation
- Urie Bronfenbrenner (humanist): human ecological systems
- Lawrence Kohlberg (humanist): values and morals
- Langston Hughes (poet): writing to learn
- Mary McLeod Bethune (educator): learning to improve
- Carol Gilligan (psychologist): a masculine society and the dilemma facing female learners
- David Elkind (humanist): readiness and learning
- Abraham Maslow (humanist): satisfying human needs
- W. E. B. DuBois (educator): intellectual achievement
- Booker T. Washington (educator): industrial and vocational learning
- Albert Bandura (behaviorist): emulation, learning from others
- B. F. Skinner (behaviorist): rewards and learning
- Howard Gardner (visionary): multiple intelligences
- Daniel Goleman (visionary): emotional intelligence

The preceding list of child-development theorists illustrates the nuances, complexities, and perceptions associated with learning. In preparing the information for this essay, the writer gleaned his educational perceptions from R. Murray Thomas's *Comparing Theories of Child Development* (1985); Thomas Armstrong's *Seven Kinds of*

Smart (1993); Daniel Goleman's audio renaissance cassette *Emotional Intelligence* (1995); and *The New Illustrated Volumes: The Columbia Encyclopedia* (1979).

In summary, I strongly feel that children define themselves and learn best when responsible parents and teachers encourage them to have high expectations and at the same time genuinely express concerns for their well-being. In doing so, these adults recognize that a child represents not only 100 billion cells of physical mass but a universe of perpetual and persistent optimism. Then how do today's young people learn about their world of vicissitudes and themselves? Frankly speaking, children learn from understanding knowledge and discovering the truth about life. Now, that was a QUANTUM LEAP into learning! In the words of educator Ambrose E. Brazelton, "I may be little, but I'm big inside."

Simple Pleasures, and
It Is Really Up to Me:
RESOLUTIONS FOR LIFE

Today in our society of trepidation, hopelessness, and vicissitudes, we can still enjoy a variety of simple pleasures. For example, the daily sunshine provides warmth and vision for both blind and sighted individuals, and also for those people who are blinded by reckless ambition, insatiable greed, unquenchable hatred, and grandiose attitudes. Yes, my friends, we must never forget the pure taste of the Earth's precious waters and the freshness of air, which cool our dry palates and uncurl the unrestrained waves of sweat on our foreheads. Simple pleasures in our lifetime—a walk in the park, true friendship, unconditional love, the birth of a child, uncontrollable laughter—are indeed boundless, undeniably pervasive, very routine, and available to all who use their five senses and emotional intelligence during the journey through life.

However, the days in which we live often appear disappointing to many men and women, and boys and girls. Seemingly for some people, the human frailties of the flesh, spirit, and mind are insidiously overwhelming—a burdensome lifestyle. From time to time, mankind is troubled, besieged, and inundated with the news about persons being overly stressed, unmercifully displaced, perniciously victimized, violently uprooted, and savagely murdered. So true; nevertheless, and through every vitriolic circumstance, one cannot underestimate the power of potential happiness or kinetic optimism.

Now take, for instance, a youngster who is last at bat in a Little League baseball championship game with the score 0 to 3, two outs, and is faced with the possibility of losing or winning the ball game. In the final inning of play, this particular batter has 3 balls and 2 strikes called on him without ever having swung his heavy bat. The nervous hitter and all of the baseball fans in the ballpark realize that if a home run is hit, the runners on the bases plus the hitless batter will score (four come-from-behind runs) to win the game and championship. The flawless pitcher on the mound for the opposing team senses the uneasiness of this worried slugger and decides to throw a breaking pitch (curve ball). Much to the surprise of everyone, the anxious batter, now perspiring with beads of profuse sweat, makes a deliberate attempt to hit the invisible baseball and sees the gift of victory in a time of disbelief. Without a doubt, the Little League scenario clearly embraces and unequivocally epitomizes the courageous performance of simplicity.

As I mentioned earlier, laughter is an effective simple pleasure. Greek writer Menander (342–291 BC), who wrote the famous play *Curmudgeon* about a satirical form of entertainment called New Comedy, made laughter a central theme in many of his theatrical works involving the throes of despair and the throngs of life (tragedies, disappointments, setbacks, lovers, complexities, various family problems). And guess what? A number of research reports from biochemists and physiologists suggest that laughing and smiling do help to increase the levels of endorphins and peptides (amino acids) in our brains. These chemically based, simple pleasures seem to raise the threshold of pain during one's painful experiences. Therefore, in this new year and years to come, make every effort to motivate yourselves to smile, laugh, and celebrate these simple pleasures—the touch of a child's hand, the passing of time, that special moment, giving directions to someone who is lost, the enjoyment of a raindrop, the finding of a penny. In the songs of composer Duke Ellington and vocalist Aretha Franklin, respectively speaking, "take the 'A' train" and "respect yourself." Remember, simple pleasures! Please go out and have a balmy and exciting day. Goodbye, and I will see you in the morning.

NOTICE

To see other books written by Charles L. Singleton or to check out other books written by other authors, you may visit www.allencopublishing2.com and browse through the website to see what books may interest you.

NOTES

NOTES

NOTES

NOTES

NOTES

NOTES

9 780976 223276